Double Stop Beginnings

for the Cello

Book One

by Cassia Harvey

CHP220

©2011 by C. Harvey Publications All Rights Reserved.

6403 N. 6th Street

Philadelphia, PA 19126

www.charveypublications.com

Suggestions to Improve Sound

1. Press the fingers of the left hand down firmly.
2. Make sure the fingers are in tune.
    Fourth finger needs special attention so that the sound is not flat.
3. Balance the bow evenly across the two strings in each double stop.
4. Play *mf* or *mp* so you can hear the notes clearly.
5. Keep the bow moving across the strings; don't get stuck.

WEEK 1

Double Stop Beginnings for the Cello, Book One

Double Stop Exercise 1

Cassia Harvey

CHP220 ©2011 C. Harvey Publications All Rights Reserved.

www.charveypublications.com

Listen to make the notes blend.

Double Stops with String Crossing

Fiddle Tune: Devil's Dream

Double Stop Exercise 2

WEEK 2

Note: Curve your fingers so that you do not touch the top string.

Listen to make the notes blend.

Scales in Double Stops

Fiddle Tune: Cripple Creek

Stephen Foster's Tune: Oh Susannah

Double Stop Exercise 3   **WEEK 3**

Listen to make the notes blend.

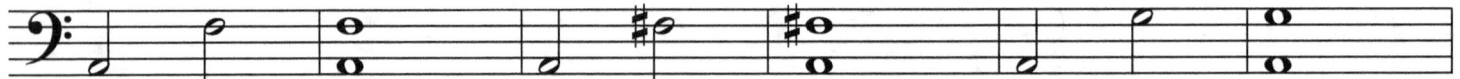

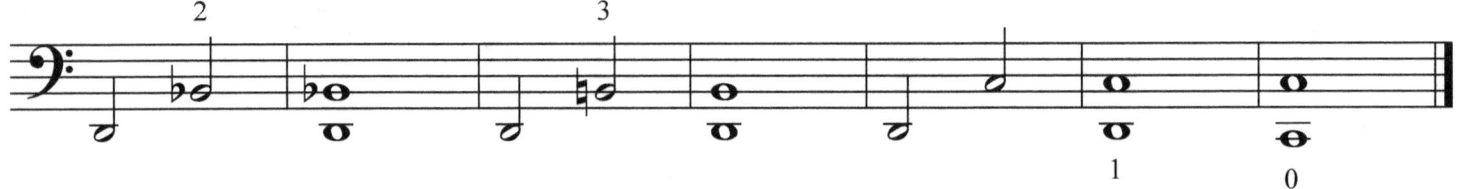

Switching fingers and strings

Fiddle Tune: Arkansas Traveler

Double Stop Exercise 4 — WEEK 4

Double Stop Beginnings for the Cello, Book One

Listen to make the notes blend.

Double Stops on Arpeggios

C major

F major

Fiddle Tune: Soldier's Joy

Double Stop Exercise 5 — WEEK 5

Listen to make the notes blend.

Double Stop Slurs

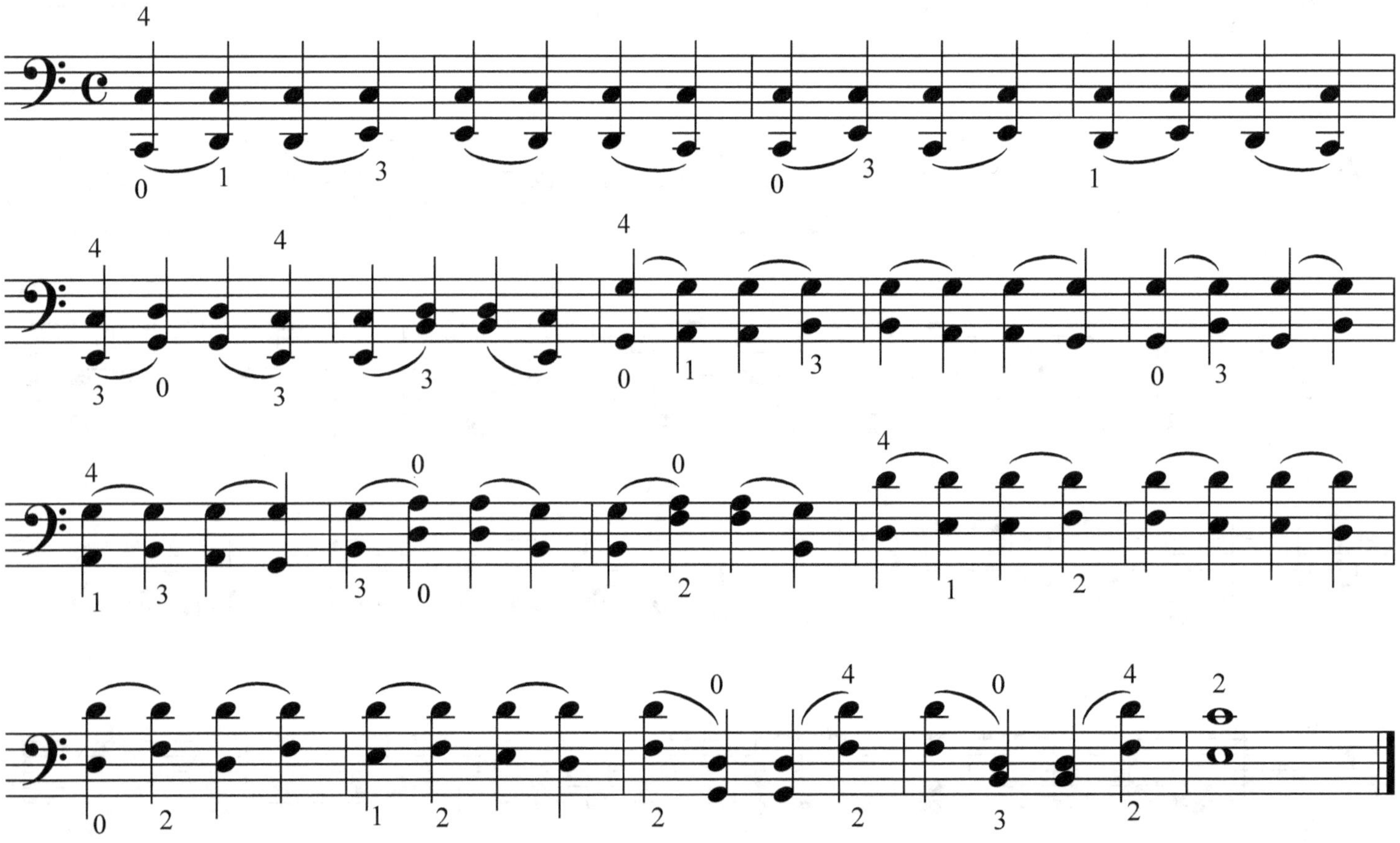

Double Stop Beginnings for the Cello, Book One 17

Fiddle Tune: Polly Wolly Doodle

Fiddle Tune: The Honeycomb Rock

CHP220 ©2011 C. Harvey Publications All Rights Reserved. www.charveypublications.com

Listen to make the notes blend.

Etude by Spohr

Irish Fiddle Tune: The Galway Piper

Irish Fiddle Tune: John Ryan's Polka

Double Stop Exercise 7

WEEK 7

Double Stop Beginnings for the Cello, Book One

* Flatten or "bar" the finger across the A and D strings.

CHP220 ©2011 C. Harvey Publications All Rights Reserved. www.charveypublications.com

Double Stop Beginnings for the Cello, Book One

Listen to make the notes blend.

Chords

This is how to play chords of three notes.

These two measures are played the same.

English Folk Tune

Fiddle Tune: Turkey in the Straw

24

WEEK 8

Double Stop Exercise 8

CHP220 ©2011 C. Harvey Publications All Rights Reserved.

Double Stop Beginnings for the Cello, Book One

www.charveypublications.com

Fiddle Tune: Mount Hills

Barbarini's Tambourine

Fiddle Tune: Colonel Gordon's Minuet

www.ingramcontent.com/pod-product-compliance
Lightning Source LLC
Chambersburg PA
CBHW051432070526
44584CB00023B/3685